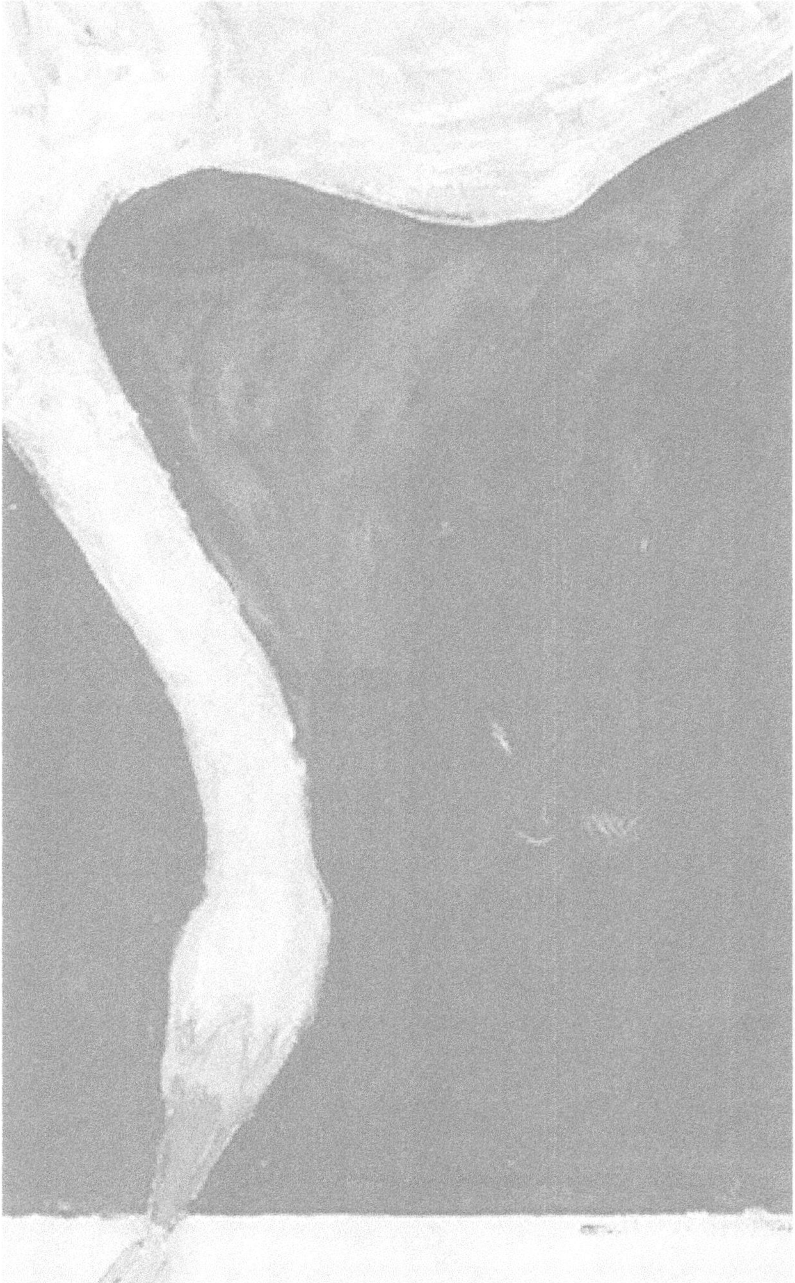

The Water Between Us

The Water Between Us

Gillian Ebersole

Winner of the Charlotte Mew Prize

HEADMISTRESS PRESS

Copyright © 2021 by Gillian Ebersole
All rights reserved.

ISBN 978-1-7335345-8-1

This book may not be reproduced, in whole or in part, including illustrations, in any form (beyond that permitted by Sections 107 and 108 of the U.S. Copyright Law and except by reviewers for the public press), without written permission from the publishers.

Cover art: Hilma af Klint, Group IX/SUW, The Swan (Svanen), No. 1, 1915. From The SUW/UW Series, 1915. Oil on canvas, 59 1/16 x 59 1/16 inches (150 x 150 cm). The Hilma af Klint Foundation, Stockholm, HaK 149. Public Domain.
Cover & book design by Mary Meriam

PUBLISHER
Headmistress Press
60 Shipview Lane
Sequim, WA 98382
Telephone: 917-428-8312
Email: headmistresspress@gmail.com
Website: headmistresspress.blogspot.com

for John Todd

Contents

Moon Prayer	1
I hope everything I have lost is under a bookshelf in the corner of heaven	2
queering queer	4
Exit Wounds	6
On Philippa Foot and Virtual Memorials	7
From the Summer of '08	8
Backyard Haibun	9
Annex Nocturne	10
I don't know the names of the people next door	11
these are the things I will remember	12
Venice Beach	14
Breakup Fish and Stolen Furniture	15
I wish the missing was symmetrical	17
woozy	18
Duplex	19
alternate universe in which I am unafraid of my mother	20
Pussy Riot	21
queer nocturne	23
on being perceived	25
Vestido	26
Retrograde	27
Cancer Season	28
55 Rue de l'Abbé Groult	29
friday the thirteenth	30
Writhing or Dancing	31
best friend	32
In the Crook of the Elbow	34
A mentor describes my work as queer	35
I don't know much about palmistry, but I am close friends with Fate	36
Notes	39
About the Author	40
Acknowledgments	41

Moon Prayer

The moon is a fingernail, spilling slivers of gin onto the counter. The silver liquid runs down the cabinets and drips onto the floor. Fingernail clippings accumulate in little echoes on the linoleum. A bible lies crumpled in the corner, wordless. She slumps on the couch, wearing a twisted dress, a body fragile as a pillar of salt, blown to ash. The darkness seeps in finger tendrils, curling through the open window. A siren blares. A crucifix grins. I cannot sleep because the silence grates at my ears. *Please,* I begged the fog to lift, *let me see the moonlight.*

I hope everything I have lost is under a bookshelf in the corner of heaven

Nothing is more practical than finding God, that is, than falling in a love in a quite absolute, final way.
~ Pedro Arrupe

I've yet to find the appropriate tension
between sword and surrender.

Once when we were arguing
about religion, you asked me –
do you even love God?

A professor I loved died
after consoling me with an email,
a gentle elbow, and a nudged chair.

It is hard for me to trust a religion
that speaks in clichés.

My mother is teaching the alphabet
to a small boy in a spare bedroom.
Every few minutes he sings a song
he made up just for her.

I am obsessed with disproving
the existence of a good God,
which means I wear my problems
as emblems, add world tragedies
to a jean jacket overflowing
with iron-on cynicism, keep
a running list of evil people
who do not deserve grace.

I win a gift card and buy candles,
try to burn sacred into my room.
I'm desperate for the smell of funerals
and incense and Sunday mornings.

What is on the other side of metal and a white flag?

If you asked, I'd lay down my sword
at your altar, spend my life kneeling
until I believed love could heal the bruises.

queering queer

when I sat in cold metal desks under a crucifix,
I read the vocabulary word *queer*
        defined as *strange; odd*. I never questioned
        what this word might mean – queer.

but marriage featured a young woman and a balding
man. catholicism is the antithesis
        of *strange; odd* even though a god three persons
        in one love triangle is rather queer.

now, I laugh a little, thinking about high school theater,
pastel-colored hair, and dating boys
        who became gay men. how we all felt safe
        in the backstage closet, a left-out definition of queer.

he held me so softly most days, and I wanted him
to grab me and shove me into a wall and tell
        me that he needed me. it was so fucked up really.
        I came from relationships that weren't queer,

where bruises and black lips meant I love you,
so when he kissed my forehead, I just knew
        he would leave me. I found a polaroid of him
        kissing another woman at the club. queer.

I remember those early nights leaning into the Paris
air, drunk on wine and our own trauma.
        she stepped into our friendship gently, when we donned
        pixie cuts and pantsuits to look queer.

look, I never looked for her love. I thought the grocery
store runs and failed recipes sprung
      from our mutual distaste for college men
        and our habit of collecting words for poetry, like queer.

when she told me she loved me, she stopped speaking,
only alcohol would break her silence,
      making her lurch with slurred insults. she set fires
        and burned me for the way I wore queer.

she took one yes and made it origami, dumped a thousand
paper cranes on my doorstep when I asked
      to be alone, stuffed me in the cardboard box
        that held the paper, made me the queer

she wanted. my roommate asks me which men
I want to fuck and I vomit. she asks me which women
      I want to fuck and I vomit. I don't want to fuck
        anyone. I have been violenced by queer.

so many labels, with none that seem to fit quite right,
trying to squeeze myself into an identity
      like an old pair of jeans but my genes
        always seem to lie to me. still, I like the fit of queer.

Exit Wounds

I left the Church
with half of my hope; a decent
singing voice, a closet full
of dowdy dresses, twelve
plastic rosaries, a confirmation
saint to watch over me, and an unhealthy
sense of guilt, given to me by a priest
who asked if I'd participated in any
inappropriate touching.

At the time, I cried.
Now, I grow nauseous
at the irony of his accusation.

God must have a sick sense of humor
giving humans a responsibility so fragile
yet we're children with buttered hands —
dishes slip from our grasp in the kitchen.

It scares me to think I'll feel this much
pain my whole life
which is, perhaps, an explanation
for my appearance in the pews every Sunday.

On Philippa Foot and Virtual Memorials

If grief could be solved with a good book and a few moments spent standing in the rain, I'd be dragging whole libraries into this summer shower. I'm driving on the 405, and it is pouring. I visit two art museums in one day, wandering among abstract paintings so big my neck hurts. At this point, you're still alive. I wish I could be satisfied as a simple yellow streak of paint, but I want to be the whole fucking ceiling of the Sistine Chapel. I can hear you telling me to decide. I've never been indecisive, but it takes a whole lot of energy to put my mind to something. Don't you get tired? The next time it rains, I am rocking my knees at my chest in my twin-sized childhood bed. It has a princess canopy for god's sake. You're dying, and I am sleeping in polka dot sheets. I find out you have cancer at 6pm and you're dead by midnight. My friend calls me because she sees the news online. We cry silently on the phone for an hour. There's lightning outside my window and a pile of tissues in my lap. I make a list of people I wish died instead of you. The trolley problem is not as difficult now. I feel guiltier laughing than playing guillotine in my head. It's hard to imagine you resting now. Maybe the place where you are doesn't require sleep. I hope it rains there.

From the Summer of '08

The fox in August. I still dream:
the plastic pool. Icy hose water.
      Mosquito bites the size of golf
balls, covered in toothpaste.

The air smells of ice cream,
blacktop, and sweat. A skinned
      knee. Popsicle fireworks explode.
Stained fingertips on swing sets.

Lying face-up in the grass, I escape
to muggy nights. Tracing paw
      prints left by the flaming fox.
The plastic pool floats in the orange sky.

Backyard Haibun

The first time you saw a rabbit shot, you cried big alligator tears. Red splatters in the snow floated before your eyes. That yard was our home, the place where I crowned you king of the trees along the fence we would climb, tearing our shirts on the needles, rolling between our fingers the sticky residue from sap. You breathed dragon fire in my ear, and I ran, buoyed by the shimmery August heat, stopped only by the wheeze of high altitude. We befriended the fox beneath the porch – that sleek fence-jumper whose flash of red made us dizzy with laughter. How many afternoons did we spend building homes for the fairies in the bushes before making our own out of igloo ice cubes and ponderosa brush? Those years I believed I was a mermaid, you, a dragon, and we swung the tire swing to enter our kingdom of cows. My tears blur the memory of those alligators you shed for that rabbit, in that yard, when your world was not so dark. I would give anything to watch you in the field, running toward the mountains, toward the sunset tinged indigo and orange, sidewalk chalk on our fingertips, little grass-stained knees

collapsing side by
side by night fall when the cool
earth forgives our fire.

Annex Nocturne

You see, the moon bleeds
daffodils through the windows,
drizzles butter on the wall at dusk,
coughs up opal beads of light
caught between the blinds.

Ants crawl across the top
of the loveseat
where your toe indents
remain on the arms
from the nights you curled
around a book.

The moon noses the stale
red wine on the counter
and laps up blackberry
gloam instead.

Did you know the windowsill
cactus is named Amy?

She casts a lavender shadow
on the floor and leans toward
the stained yellow wall,
oblivious to the moonlight.

You'd probably ask if the ants need coats.

I don't know the names of the people next door

You never sang for me did you
did you think the bridge would separate
us from curtains and mirrors
and the 5 o'clock light streams
through the corner window

I will close the blinds again
and count the crows
on neighboring houses
with people we do not know inside
clutching at their blankets

the fires are talkative and the snow
quiet the moment is only us
and not us we are never alone
or as alone as we want to be

we fill the emptiness with music
let the radio blare on in the night
you know I can sleep through anything

these are the things I will remember

arugula, adagio, analog clocks
at the barre wilting
black leotard by the window wind
Berlin blues tucked into his collar
chef of *coupés* and *glissades*
combo platter including a *manèges* and *fouettés*
desperado, why don't you come to your senses?
don't clean up the carpet dancing
early mornings on frosted marley
every class a cracked open ribcage
filled with the fire of belonging
filled with the fire of an empty theater
gathered
grieving
happenstance of gratitude or tragedy
he made me sing
I'm not afraid of anything
I am afraid of everything
joke's on him
jeté en tournant
knots in calves
knuckles cracked
linger after class
loiter before
Martha Graham is moving out (thank god)
mirrors stare until curtains close
neither fifth nor third
noises noticed in photos
only one cartwheel
or overdose

psychologist of *petite allegro*
pirouette in the hallways
quirked hands folded
question after question
relevé, revérénce, rond de jambe
resistance made plain in
six hours per week
stoptime sweat flinging through the air
tendu in four directions, sixteen times
thrown off a bridge (for Twyla Tharp)
underneath all this is love
unspoken
violins scream
violence of the cellular kind
we are separated
will I ever waltz again?
xo – *this is not the end*
xo – *it sure seems like it*
you are the song drifting on the wind
your *épaulment* remains in my shoulders
zealot to the end
zero doubt about that.

Venice Beach

The dingy canals choke and sputter.

White bridges span the water
and I am caught by the texture
of your hand in mine –
the callus on your index finger

tinges my memory. Regret
distracts me from looking
between your teeth. The radio
thumps to the fidgety beat
of your fist on the dash.

When the sun sets, you wander.
I wish my glasses
would fog up around you.
Then, you would never have
seen me weep for the water between us.

Breakup Fish and Stolen Furniture

x.

In the bar, we both avoid eye contact. There are pride flags everywhere and you pretend not to notice when I ask if I can take a few home, hang one on my porch, use another as a bedspread, wrap myself in the third after I shower.

ix.

Before the evening ends, we wander along the edge of a cliff. You grab my hand to keep me from falling, then abandon me to tumble down the dirt anyway. In Los Angeles, in France, on the quiet trails in Colorado, when you post on Instagram, I think about your hands and pray.

viii.

You like to hear about my research. There is a paper about a man who choreographs for ballet companies using blackface. Another about dance as gender performance. I don't tell you I am choreographing about you. There is a duet between two women who are afraid to touch each other.

vii.

Six years is a long time and not at all. I fear you will always see me as a child.

vi.

Together, stuffed. I knew you would be the one to leave. I buy you vinyls and plane tickets. There would never be enough music to keep your attention. We took a drive to escape the goodbye. I hid everything I love in your dashboard.

v.

Rainy porches. Calling your name like I am unafraid, breathing in pollution as perfume. When the stars emerge from behind the clouds, we lie on the roof, catching the moisture in our joints, using the rain as an excuse to touch.

iv.

I've come to love your fidgeting. You pace around the kitchen while I collapse like a tired horse. You buy vegetables from the farmer's market but leave them to rot.

iii.

Things we talked about: opera, camping, how we feel about our siblings, avoiding coming out to our parents, how religion is both captor and captive, enneagram compatibility, preferred type of pen, falling in love with straight women, Southwest Airlines.

ii.

Things we didn't talk about: actually coming out, Instagram, where you'd sleep when you come to visit, overdoses, if I could hold onto your waist when we rode your motorcycle, churches, how many of your friends you've dated, stubborn avoidance.

i.

We can't forgive each other for the past. I stand outside your door but still cannot bring myself to knock.

I wish the missing was symmetrical

I wonder if you have ever checked our zodiac compatibility.
I can't stop thinking about your blue eyes, peanut butter,
and my last London fog. My tears are as bitter as Earl Grey,

and my mind as cloudy. Do the stars align?
Our coffee shop is closed, which means you are alone,
making coffee barefoot in your kitchen.

I used your bathroom last time I was over, and I discovered
we have the same face wash. Cut to a montage of domestic bliss.
Miles away, I'm back to praying broken rosaries.

I wish we were a circle instead of two points in time.
I want roses, yellow ones, and I want you
to hang a pride flag from your window.
If I wasn't stained purple, I'd be stronger.

woozy

she said I was like the wind. my life is a string and I wanted to kiss her knees to pass the time. I wanted to stop speaking my declarations as if they were questions. when she sat on her desk we were both reeling. it takes more than a bottle of tito's to fix a dead fish and an unmade bed.

please hold me, I'm sorry. please hold me, we will trade small notebooks in the second of darkness before the bathroom light turns on. I want to be like your cassette collection or at least in your car long enough to drive the length of the pacific coast with you. I want burnt blankets and weighted mornings and the space between your bed and the garden. I regret every unknocked door. between capital and lowercase letters I try to decipher your flannel – just tell me to go. it would be easier, really.

as if this were a postcard, breathe in my faded perfume and rip it up.

Duplex

I have never been anyone's favorite.
I believe in holding hands when I pray.

> I believe in holding your hands to pray –
> your fingers make me worship soggy grass.

Your fingers make me prickle like fresh grass,
you wore a little makeup yesterday.

> I wore some blue mascara yesterday.
> For you, I would hide all my cinnamon.

For me, you would use all the cinnamon.
You always forget to water your plants,

> but I'll never forget to water the plants.
> You text me *I love you* two years late –

I never answer til two years later.
I have never been anyone's favorite.

alternate universe in which I am unafraid of my mother

when a professor describes me as maternal, I don't listen. instead, I wear fishnets and a red leather skirt to the next class. I seduce him with lipsticked confidence. I am twenty-two and I hate children. once, my roommate crowned me the mom of our friend group, so I forgot the keys on purpose. a friend told me I would be a good mother, so I made an angry face at a baby in the grocery store. when my friends from high school get engaged, I learn iron smithing, forge a sword, slice men with that sword. I taught myself to cook by playing with the stove. my mother says she wishes I were thinner, so I throw the scale out the window. she says there is no education to become a mom, so I leave parenting books under her pillow. she says I will never find a husband, so I start dating women. she says I talk too much, so I record myself screaming and set it as her ringtone. my mother says this is not the meaning of unafraid. when my mother says I should dress modestly and I buy lingerie, she calls this a phase. but left over from the other universe are hours and hours spent crying in a pillow, wishing she would tell me I'm beautiful, and here, they are just hours. here, they are a floor-length sparkly gown. here, they are a day without counting calories. here, they are nights when I stay awake until the sun kisses my cheeks. here, they are a weekend when I forget to do laundry because I am laughing in a bar. here, I hand an hour to a woman as she staggers on sunset boulevard. I tuck one into my best friend's bed, send my brother a few in the mail. I do not make a scene on mother's day. I do not lie. I do not hide my tattoos. I do not call home. I do not come home. I do not ask for her opinion. my mother tells me she is tired, and she is tired. my mother tells me she wishes I were different, and I smile. I have made my body my home.

Pussy Riot
Céder un peu c'est capituler beaucoup.

My body has been gerrymandered
to fit the schemes of the latest white
man in office. He gouges so deep
my period skips four months
and when it comes, I bleed for weeks
because my healthcare costs
as much as my rent and it does not cover
birth control even though half
the time I like women better than men,
but this too is a sin.

The man screams at me until the words
queer and *asexual* catch in my throat –
I can't bear to bring them to fruition
because having sex and not having
sex somehow mark me as tainted either way.

I have a sticker on my laptop that reads
I'm not sorry about your fragile masculinity
and the man attacks me for it in my favorite
coffeeshop. I send him the Wikipedia page
on masculinity in response, and three weeks
later he returns and asks me if I work
out, how did I get that body, would
I like to talk more about his masculinity?

When I tell people I had to leave
my favorite coffeeshop because of this man,
they roll their eyes. My coworker laughs
and says he'll believe it when he sees
it. My friends tell me to go to the polls,
but the man sends my ballot back. I hear

the man in the apartment next to me say
somebody's gonna get raped

and I am blinded as my first boyfriend shoves
me into a wall and I learn how to make
myself as small as possible, sinking into
the La-Z-Boy chair as his unwanted tongue
inches down my bare neck. I find
a sobbing woman in the bathroom.

I see myself flinch when the boy I love
goes to touch me without asking, and I wrap
the asexual flag around my shoulders
because then, at least, some people leave me
alone. Next to me, on the subway a mother
tells her 5-year-old daughter to close her legs
and my 11-year-old friend gets dress-coded
for her less-than-three-fingers-wide tank top straps.

Lady Gaga plays in the restaurant and I have
to excuse myself to take deep breaths, heaving
over a random bathroom sink. The man sang
"Bad Romance" when he unhooked my bra
in 6th grade Spanish class. A drunk girl
staggers into his bedroom. My best
friend numbers her encounters with the man
reaching her fingers and toes.

I scream about a president who grabs pussies
and I cry over a Supreme Court appointment,
watching yet another stock of men take up
the robes of the priesthood, and I am exhausted.

I do not think the man will ever understand
to give in a little is to give up everything.

queer nocturne

my straight friends complain
I scare the boys away.

and by boys, they mean eligible,
young, and attractive men.

they aren't wrong – the ring
of space around us at the club

is interrupted only by the slurs
of men too drunk to be eligible.

then, my friends melt into queerness,
claim me as their girlfriend

by clutching my arm, pull
me in close enough to feel safe.

later, I am the paparazzi,
taking photos of my friends

posing in the dim bar light.
one says *you'd be such a good boy*

friend in a moscow mule drawl
and I laugh. I'm not offended.

I'm not offended, I tell myself.
I know she won't remember

asking me to dance tomorrow
and I'll try to forget it too.

there are a thousand photos
of her in my camera roll.

on being perceived

You dress me in pearls and I'm femme, but a chain of paper clips makes me butch. Strip me, call me a slut – I'm at the mercy of you yanking a dress over my head – tape my mouth shut, tie my wrists with those pearls. Thigh high boots will not make me more of a woman. Draw a heart on my breast with a marker – I'm too cold for you anyway. Inside my chest is a wheelbarrow, a spindle, a piece of paper, an equation. My elbow is a puzzle piece without a place to fit. My shoulder blades take flight, tearing off my back to rip holes in ceilings and last year's paper snowflakes. In the sky, there are crows and a bridge to a dinner party with Audre Lorde, bell hooks, Roxane Gay, and Claire Bishop. You're not there to see me break pearl necklaces and sleep in a tub of cocoa butter. I bleed rose petals every month and plant them in the ground. My shirt pockets overflow with butterflies and cross-hatched doodles. I finally get that rose tattoo my mother will hate. I tear out my infected ear piercing and grow a maze of leaves on my legs. There are no more masks, middle fingers, or AK-47s. I can walk alone in the night.

Vestido

I wear a plaid jumper
to my first Spanish class.
Derek climbs under my desk
to look up my skirt.

I tell myself I hate dresses.
My mother returns the once-worn
plaid jumper. I buy dress pants
and sit with my legs open.

When I wear a dress for prom,
my mother cries. My date
unsuccessfully tries to stick his hands
up the floor-length gown.

Billy Porter wears a tuxedo
fashioned into a dress
to the 91st Academy Awards.
Is this liberation?

The Spanish word for dress
is masculine.

Retrograde

I don't often wish I could change
the movement of my heart –
each flutter as rash and impulsive
as the last, but I long
for the incomplete melody
that you are
the clumsy half-ripe avocado
sunset to-do list maker
polaroid taker.

I think about redoing this life
so you could end up with your head in my lap
turning back time so we could be kinder
my fingers holding your tshirt
and you singing
to me, fretting the guitar
in my ear until I sleep
every night a poem of defiance
every kiss an act of treason
proving our former future selves
we didn't shatter too sharply
when we broke
our edges would fit together
instead of cutting each other.

Cancer Season

That year was the worst year of your whole life.
So dark you sunburned yourself on the beach
to try to feel warmth again. Blister, strife.
The holes outnumbered sea glass and peaches,

and I could not devise a way to dig
you out. You built toothpick gossip ladders –
those straw nothings crumbled, and dirt sprig
tears could not make your eyeliner sadder.

Wearing rainbow socks and hotel slippers,
you now make tea in the kitchen at dawn,
pale skin under the moon, phase worshipper,
the smile on your face no longer withdrawn.

The peach pits and sunburn scars weren't wasted –
we crave the things we have not yet tasted.

55 Rue de l'Abbé Groult

You squish next to me on the metro,
wearing your slightly yellowed
but forever-crisp white button
down. I catch a whiff of your musky
forehead sweat before you disappear
into the Châtelet tunnels, and I am left
leaning against the cool windowpane.

I wander narrow alleys in the mornings,
stumbling on every foggy cobblestone.
I burn my tongue on café au lait
(even though I hate coffee)
trying to remember the taste of you.
I buy a pack of cigarettes and leave it unopened
in my underwear drawer. I fling open
the windows to my apartment at dusk
to see the rose clouds, wearing nothing
but that white button down. I try every brand
of sauvignon blanc from the grocery
at the end of the block until my blood runs
clear. I spread raspberry jam on a day-old baguette
and make farfalle with salt at 10pm. I sleep
in your shirt. I drink English breakfast in your mug,
I breathe in my neighbor's cigarette smoke,
and I miss you.

There are cigarette butts on the sidewalk,
crusts of yesterday's nicotine rush on your collar.

friday the thirteenth

the wind is howling and I'm crying. you pull the hair out of your face but it sticks to your lips anyway. I shake my fist at the sky as we stand six feet apart. you're sick and I'm in love. these are the facts. the goodbyes involve cake, wine, and paint by number kits. my best friend wears a rush beta shirt that I stole from the roommate I hate. her blonde hairs are in my laundry. we haven't had a piece of fruit in a week. I dance in my living room. five flights are cancelled before I get back to my parents' house. they still don't know I love you. they also don't know I have tattoos – three of them. I dream about blood and the last time you wore a baseball hat backward. I cry six times in one day. we make cookies out of old bananas and instant oatmeal. I listen to Patsy Cline for 56 hours. you post about me on Instagram and delete it ten minutes later. it's 12:01 am.

Writing or Dancing

How often our foreheads have touched for the pain
of circumstances, how often my cheeks have kissed yours

as we dance. I've started singing when I walk – the sharp
pain in my ribs hurts more than my nostalgia for things unknown,

and that's a relief. I write notes on gum wrappers and you frame
them – I never expected your eyes to be doey, dewy, misty

in my presence. My chest cracks open to reveal flames. I float
on the smoke until I'm trapped by the ceiling. We reach

for the top shelf, teetering on the edge, in search of last night's
rye crumb, the pair of pants that always escapes to the back

of the closet, reaching for that picnic blanket we threw out, for mothballs,
for mouths that turn upward instead of down. You are my favorite sock.

I will never outgrow you. I unearth my worn-out black sale rack sock.
I have memorized its holes, grown accustomed to the loose elastic

around the ankle, repaired the rips between my toes. No hole is too large
for me to sew. No pattern too irregular to be deemed a dance.

best friend

you talk to crows
and always forget
your sunglasses.

you are a porcupine,
prone to prickliness
at the sight of a baby
and the barista
who always bungles
your order.

you leave your spines
all over the apartment,
a slammed door
when the music
is too loud,
what is that awful
smell?
when the bathroom
isn't cleaned on time.

you name all your plants
after song lyrics
(shin bruise, morphine, anjela)
and buy lip gloss
every time you pick
up a prescription at cvs.

my hugs make you
bristle, but you like
my poetry. I have never
laughed harder
than on our couch,
falling onto the floor.

I pick your blonde hairs
out of my laundry,
soft strings of light.

In the Crook of the Elbow

The fullness of being alive is the something that is worth burning.
~ Monica Williams

We cut your hair in the sink
of my first apartment, chopped
off six inches of weight – summer
heat blazing as we ate croissants
in bed, drank red wine dressed
in towels after showering.

Now, in your car, I writhe my socked
feet on the dashboard and you count
the eyelashes floating in the air.

Your head bobs to the music
fingers on the wheel, elbows splayed
so you have space to move your ribs,
dancing, fingers in my hair, in the air
outside, in the bag of taco bell between us.
I can taste the salt on my lips,
the soft crevices of dehydration.

How many times we have stumbled,
taken our shirts off in the heat, rolled
on the floors of museums, cursed
the sky with our eyelids, laughed
until we held each other shaking?

Your foot fits in my elbow,
my head in your armpit.

A mentor describes my work as queer

I spiral.

Was it that obvious? She meant well –
it was a compliment. She knows I am queer.
I make queer art. I write queer poems. I dance queer dances.

Will I ever write a poem
that isn't tangled in queerness?
I beg the empty theater for choreography
that doesn't look gay.

I jump with these queer legs, pirouette
through gender roles, tenderly gesture
toward my sharpened buzz cut.

After the curtain falls, I gather
the flowers from the ground, toss
the petals into the air.

I don't know much about palmistry, but I am close friends with Fate

a fortune teller read your name on the heartline
of my palm. I used to believe the road was supposed
to be barren. closets are dark and beds empty.
the classroom, a gavel. religion, a crucifixion.

if god is love then I met her in you, felt her breathe
in your ribcage, got drunk on your holy water tears.
I joined the church choir of creaky joints and bouncing
knees. at your table, there is no sacrificial lamb

and no blood but our own. god is a highchair toddler
who laughs when her feet touch the grass. in this church,
we worship refrigerator duets and unmade beds, 2am
popcorn paired with expensive wine and radio blur.

my heartline ends in a feather just between your porch
and my stubbornness. thank god for phone calls and apologies.

Notes

"these are the things I will remember": in memory of John Todd

"Venice Beach": after Georg Trakl's "In Venice"

"Breakup Fish and Stolen Furniture": this poem draws on Hala Alyan's "Wife in Reverse"

"woozy": after Raquel Isabelle de Alderete

"Duplex": after Jericho Brown

"alternate universe in which I am unafraid of my mother": inspired by Olivia Gatwood's "Alternate Universe in Which I Am Unfazed by the Men Who Do Not Love Me"

"on being perceived": after Antonius-Tín Bui's 2019 exhibition *Finding Heart* at Laband Art Gallery

About the Author

Gillian Ebersole graduated Summa Cum Laude from Loyola Marymount University in Los Angeles, California, with a dual degree in Dance and English. She is a published dance critic and researcher, as well as a dancer and choreographer. In her free time, Gillian can be found drinking earl grey tea with a splash of milk and teaching yoga. She is a sunset fanatic and paints all her bedrooms yellow. Inspired by bodies and brokenness, Gillian loves exploring what makes us human.

Acknowledgments

Thank you to the editors of the following journals, which first published these poems:

Pomona Valley Review: "queering queer", "friday the thirteenth"
Lavender Review: "woozy"

I am so thankful for Monica Williams, who gave me the opportunity to display versions of the following poems in the Thomas P. Kelly, Jr. Art Gallery exhibit *when there's nothing left to burn, you have to set yourself on fire:* "Writhing or Dancing", "In the Crook of the Elbow", "Backyard Haibun", "Cancer Season", "55 Rue de l'Abbé Groult", "best friend", "Duplex"

I am especially grateful to Vi Khi Nao for choosing my poetry in the Charlotte Mew Chapbook Contest and to Headmistress Press for finding a place for my poetry to land.

I could not have written any of these poems without the many people who have read my writing in all its horrific and glorious stages. Thank you to the Loyola Marymount University English Department, most notably, Dr. Gail Wronsky, Sarah Maclay, and Dr. Michelle Bitting for the hours of workshopping and feedback.

To my friends – especially Lauree Anne De Mattos, Ali Alderman, Madison Hansen, and Marlene Jensen – who have read all my emailed and screenshotted poetry, I thank you from the bottom of my heart.

To Abby Medlin, whose friendship sustained me through a period of immense growing pains.

To those who keep my faith alive, especially Chris de Silva, Dr. Susan Abraham, and Dr. Daniel Speak.

Finally, endless gratitude to John Todd, who believed in me when I could barely drag myself out of bed to come to ballet class. When I told him I wanted to write a book, he asked me when it would be published. I hope you are reading it now. I love you.

Headmistress Press Books

Demoted Planet - Katherine Fallon
Earlier Households - Bonnie J. Morris
The Things We Bring with Us: Travel Poems - S.G. Huerta
The Water Between Us - Gillian Ebersole
Discomfort - Sarah Caulfield
The History of a Voice - Jessica Jopp
I Wish My Father - Lesléa Newman
Tender Age - Luiza Flynn-Goodlett
Low-water's Edge - Jean A. Kingsley
Routine Bloodwork - Colleen McKee
Queer Hagiographies - Audra Puchalski
Why I Never Finished My Dissertation - Laura Foley
The Princess of Pain - Carolyn Gage & Sudie Rakusin
Seed - Janice Gould
Riding with Anne Sexton - Jen Rouse
Spoiled Meat - Nicole Santalucia
Cake - Jen Rouse
The Salt and the Song - Virginia Petrucci
mad girl's crush tweet - summer jade leavitt
Saturn coming out of its Retrograde - Briana Roldan
i am this girl - gina marie bernard
Week/End - Sarah Duncan
My Girl's Green Jacket - Mary Meriam
Nuts in Nutland - Mary Meriam & Hannah Barrett
Lovely - Lesléa Newman
Teeth & Teeth - Robin Reagler
How Distant the City - Freesia McKee
Shopgirls - Marissa Higgins
Riddle - Diane Fortney
When She Woke She Was an Open Field - Hilary Brown
A Crown of Violets - Renée Vivien tr. Samantha Pious

Fireworks in the Graveyard - Joy Ladin
Social Dance - Carolyn Boll
The Force of Gratitude - Janice Gould
Spine - Sarah Caulfield
I Wore the Only Garden I've Ever Grown - Kathryn Leland
Diatribe from the Library - Farrell Greenwald Brenner
Blind Girl Grunt - Constance Merritt
Acid and Tender - Jen Rouse
Beautiful Machinery - Wendy DeGroat
Odd Mercy - Gail Thomas
The Great Scissor Hunt - Jessica K. Hylton
A Bracelet of Honeybees - Lynn Strongin
Whirlwind @ Lesbos - Risa Denenberg
The Body's Alphabet - Ann Tweedy
First name Barbie last name Doll - Maureen Bocka
Heaven to Me - Abe Louise Young
Sticky - Carter Steinmann
Tiger Laughs When You Push - Ruth Lehrer
Night Ringing - Laura Foley
Paper Cranes - Dinah Dietrich
On Loving a Saudi Girl - Carina Yun
The Burn Poems - Lynn Strongin
I Carry My Mother - Lesléa Newman
Distant Music - Joan Annsfire
The Awful Suicidal Swans - Flower Conroy
Joy Street - Laura Foley
Chiaroscuro Kisses - G.L. Morrison
The Lillian Trilogy - Mary Meriam
Lady of the Moon - Amy Lowell, Lillian Faderman, Mary Meriam
Irresistible Sonnets - ed. Mary Meriam
Lavender Review - ed. Mary Meriam

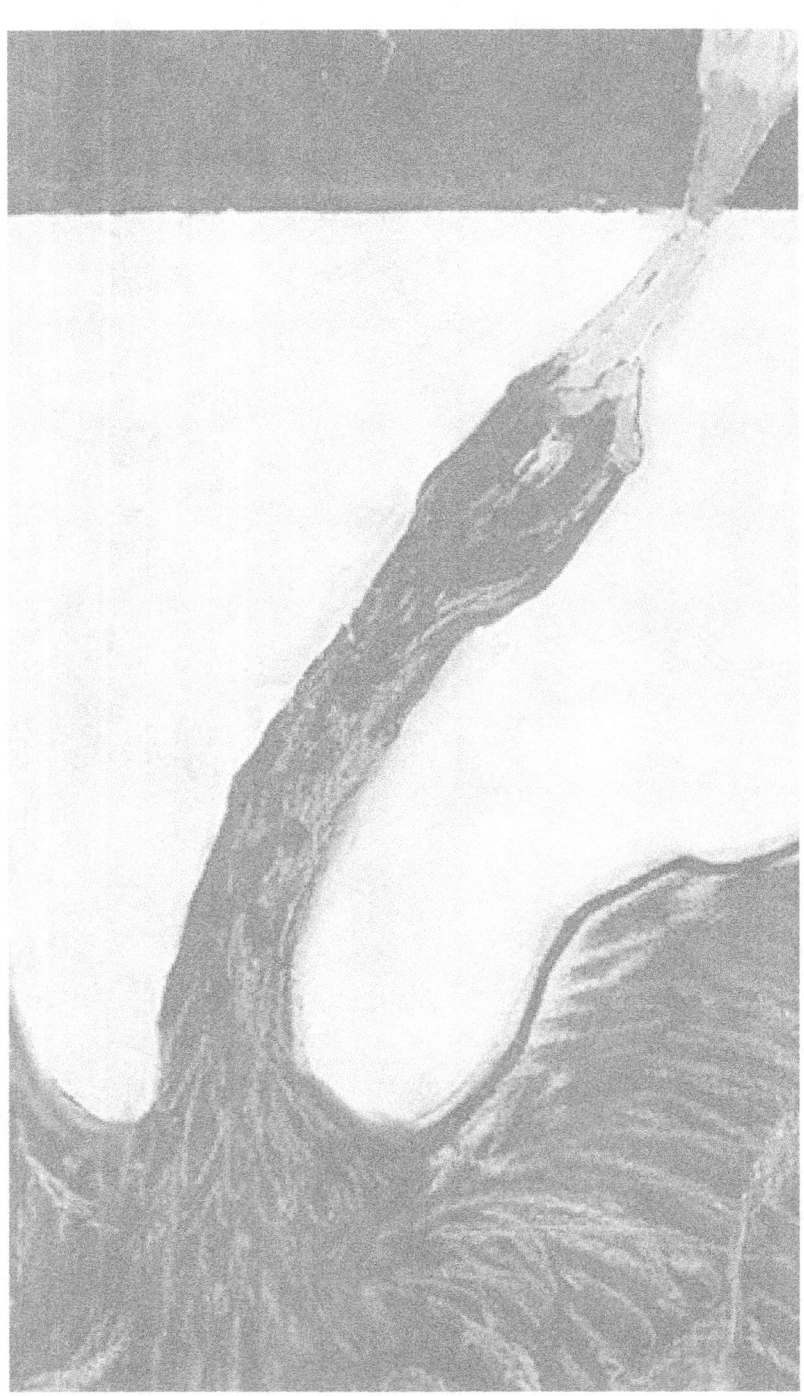

www.ingramcontent.com/pod-product-compliance
Lightning Source LLC
Chambersburg PA
CBHW060221050426
42446CB00013B/3131